Fantastic Mr. Fox

Roald Dahl

TEACHER GUIDE

NOTE:

The trade book edition of the novel used to prepare this guide is found in the Novel Units catalog and on the Novel Units website. Using other editions may have varied page references.

Please note: We have assigned Interest Levels based on our knowledge of the themes and ideas of the books included in the Novel Units sets, however, please assess the appropriateness of this novel or trade book for the age level and maturity of your students prior to reading with them. You know your students best!

ISBN 978-1-56137-049-8

Copyright infringement is a violation of Federal Law.

© 2020 by Novel Units, Inc., St. Louis, MO. All rights reserved. No part of this publication may be reproduced, translated, stored in a retrieval system, or transmitted in any way or by any means (electronic, mechanical, photocopying, recording, or otherwise) without prior written permission from Novel Units, Inc.

Reproduction of any part of this publication for an entire school or for a school system, by for-profit institutions and tutoring centers, or for commercial sale is strictly prohibited.

Novel Units is a registered trademark of Conn Education.

Printed in the United States of America.

To order, contact your local school supply store, or:

Toll-Free Fax: 877.716.7272
Phone: 888.650.4224
3901 Union Blvd., Suite 155
St. Louis, MO 63115

sales@novelunits.com

novelunits.com

Table of Contents

Summary	3
About the Author	3
Introductory Information and Activities	3
Vocabulary Activities	14
Author's Craft	16
Eighteen Chapters	19
Chapters contain: Vocabulary Words, Discussion Questions and Activities, Predictions	
Postreading Questions	28
Postreading Extension Activities	29
Assessment	35

Skills and Strategies

Thinking
Brainstorming, classifying and categorizing, evaluating, analyzing details

Vocabulary
Prefixes/suffixes, root words

Listening/Speaking
Discussion, role play

Writing
Descriptive, figurative language, persuasive

Comprehension
Predicting, sequencing, cause/effect, propaganda, fantasy and realism, comparison/contrast, inference

Literary Elements
Character, setting, plot conflict, figurative language, fantasy

Summary of Fantastic Mr. Fox
Three mean farmers start out to get the fox who has been stealing their chickens, turkeys, and ducks for years. They try to shoot, starve, and dig him out, but to no avail. Mr. Fox is very smart and, with his wit, all the wild animals have an underground adventure and life-long banquets.

About the Author
Roald Dahl was born September 13, 1916, in Llandaff, South Wales. He died November 23, 1990. Dahl was a graduate of the British Public School, 1932. He was a fighter pilot in the Royal Air Force from 1939 until 1945. He married actress Patricia Neal in 1953. They were divorced in 1983, and Dahl married Felicity Ann Crosland. Dahl and Neal had five children: Olivia, Tessa, Theo, Ophelia, and Lucy.

Best known as the author of children's books, Dahl was also noted for his short stories for adults, and his enchanting autobiographical descriptions of growing up in England and flying in World War II. His children's fiction is known for its sudden turns into the fantastic and harsh treatment of any adults foolish enough to cause trouble for the young heroes and heroines.

Dahl began by making up stories for his own children, and these became the basis for his career as a children's writer. He felt that the story must move along quickly in order to keep the interest of children, and that an author should know what children like. He once said, "The writer for children should be unconventional and inventive." With that statement, he summarized his own work.

Introductory Information and Activities
Note:
It is not intended that everything presented in this guide be done. Please be selective and use discretion when choosing the activities you will do with the unit. The choices that are made should be appropriate for your use and your group of students. A wide range of activities has been provided so that individuals as well as groups may benefit.

Initiating Activities:
1. Brainstorm the word *fox*. What are the first things that come to your mind when you hear this word? Teacher records class responses on a large sheet of paper which will be a part of the bulletin board while the novel is read.

Brainstorm!

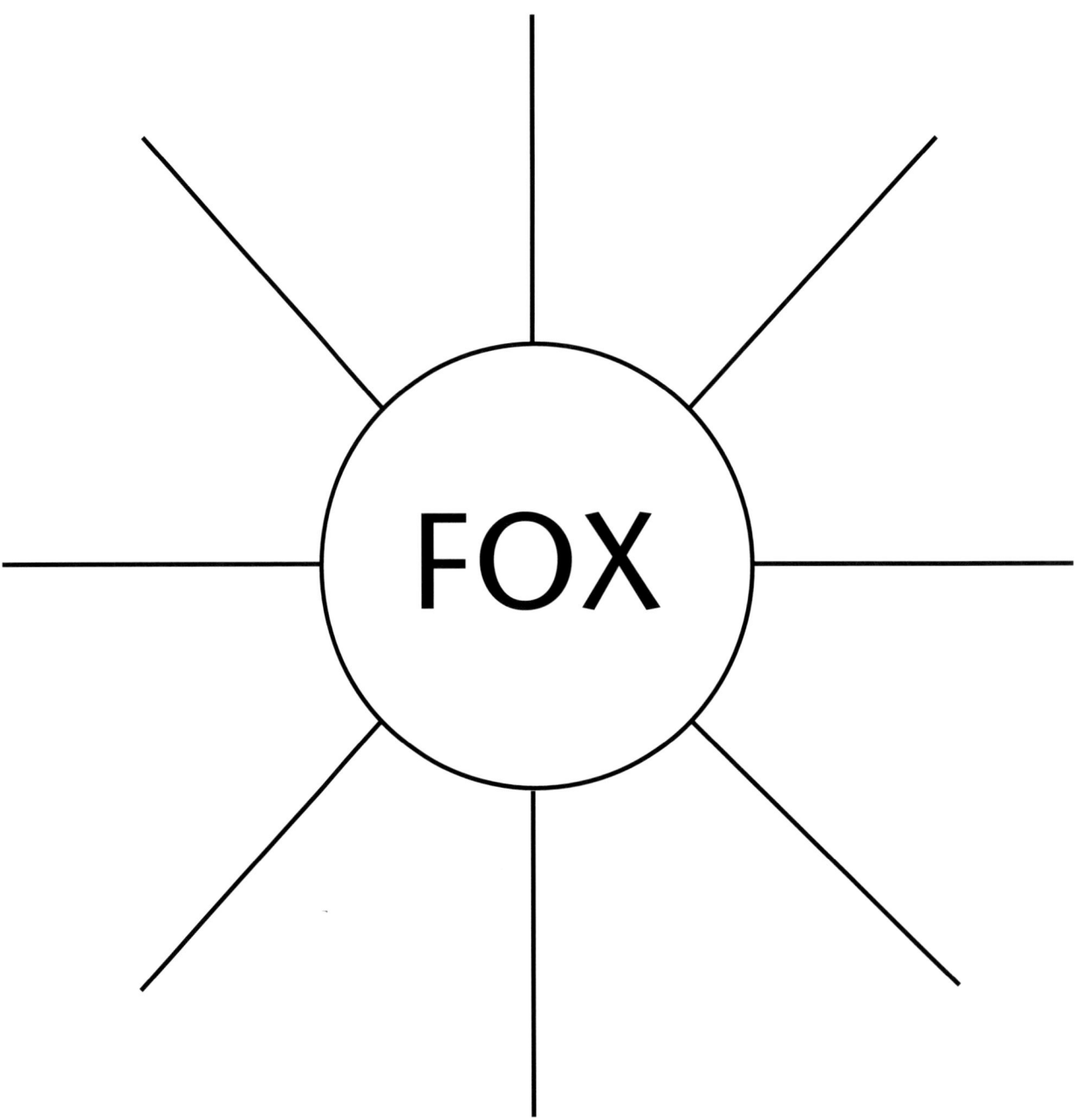

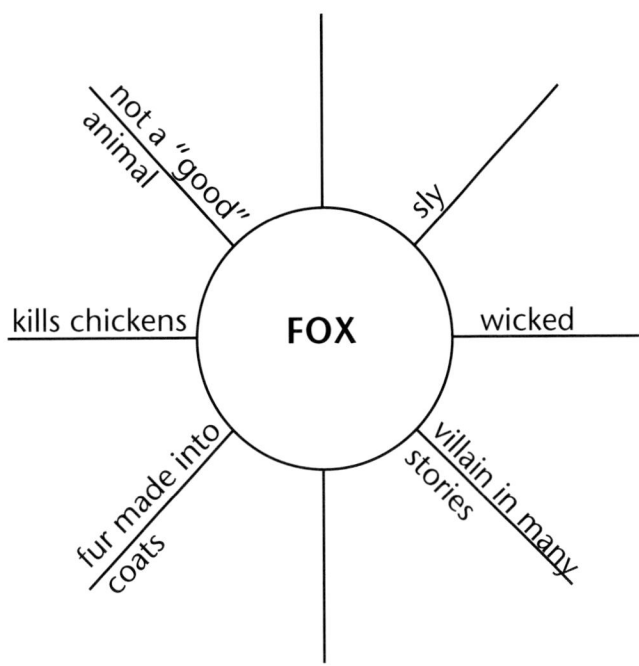

2. Look at the cover of the book. What can you predict about Mr. Fox? What does the word *fantastic* mean? How could Mr. Fox be fantastic?

Prereading Discussion Topics:
1. Facing a frightening situation: What makes you afraid? Heights, the dark, diving in deep water? Electrical storms? What do you think about when you are afraid? How do you overcome your fear? Do animals become afraid? What do you think they fear?

2. Thinking positively: Have you ever heard the expression, "the power of positive thinking"? What does it mean? Do you believe in it? If not, why not? If so, when have you seen it work for someone else? When has it worked for you?

3. Patience: Think of a time when you needed to have a lot of patience. Describe the situation. Was it difficult to have patience? Why or why not? What was the outcome? Is patience always a good thing to have?

4. Relationship of people to nature: Do you think humans have the right to kill wild animals? If so, when? What is your opinion of hunting and fishing?

Bulletin Boards:
1. Begin a research project on foxes. Post the following categories on the board: Habitat, Types of Foxes, Senses, Enemies, Defenses, Lifetime, Body, Noises, Food, Behavior, Family Life, and Foxes as Pests.

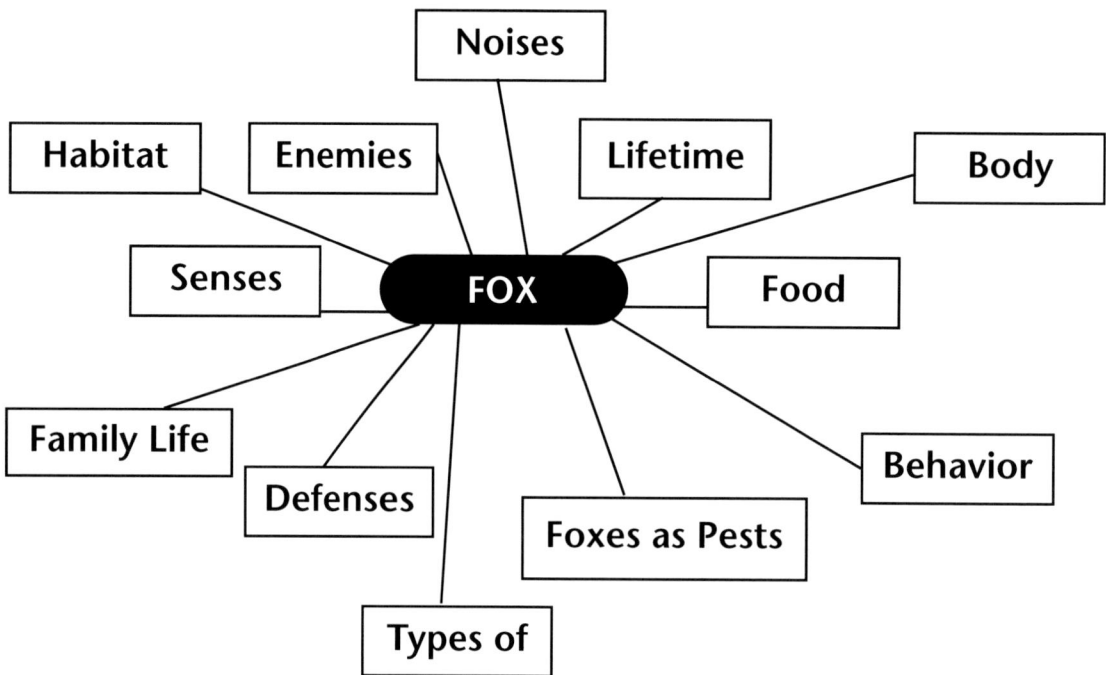

2. Journal Writing: Have students choose to identify with one of the characters—Boggis, Bunce, Bean, Mr. Fox, Mrs. Fox, or one of the Fox children—and write journal entries as the character might make throughout the story, if he could write. Entries might include one thing the character learned during the time covered by the chapter, the thing the character liked best, the thing he liked least, and what he feared. Display journal entries on a bulletin board.

3. Real Versus Make-Believe: Is *Fantastic Mr. Fox* going to be a make-believe story or a realistic story? How do you know? Use the T-diagram to discuss.

Realistic Story	Make-Believe Story
Setting—our world	Setting—not quite our world
Characters—like us	Characters—unusual
Action—could happen	Action—never could happen
Problem—could be ours	Problem—couldn't be ours

4. Cover the bulletin board with plain background paper. Divide the space into three sections. Make a collage of characters of fantasy. Place the collage in the center section of the board under the word *Fantasy*.

   As the unit progresses, ask student volunteers to write brief summaries of books that are fantasies and to place the summaries on the bulletin board. Place all of those authored by Roald Dahl in one section of the board.

```
TYPE OF BOOK:  FANTASY

ROALD DAHL              COLLAGE              OTHER AUTHORS
```

Recommended Procedure:
This book will be read one section at a time using DRTA (Directed Reading Thinking Activity) Method. This technique involves reading a section, predicting what will happen next (making good guesses) based on what has already occurred in the story. The students continue to read and everyone verifies the predictions.

Story Map:
Many stories have the same parts—a setting, a problem, a goal, and a series of events that lead to an ending or conclusion. These story elements can be placed on a story map. Just as a road map helps the driver get from one place to another, so, too, a story map leads a reader from one point to another. After reading the first chapter, what information do you have?

   *What is the setting?

   *Who are the main characters?

   *What is the problem?

There are many types of story maps. Use a class story map and then for a concluding activity, ask students to make their own type of map. (See page 10 of this guide.)

Using Predictions in the Novel Unit Approach

We all make predictions as we read—little guesses about what will happen next, how the conflict will be resolved, which details given by the author will be important to the plot, which details will help to fill in our sense of a character. Students should be encouraged to predict, to make sensible guesses. As students work on predictions, these discussion questions can be used to guide them: What are some of the ways to predict? What is the process of a sophisticated reader's thinking and predicting? What clues does an author give us to help us in making our predictions? Why are some predictions more likely than others?

A predicting chart is for students to record their predictions. As each subsequent chapter is discussed, you can review and correct previous predictions. This procedure serves to focus on predictions and to review the stories.

Use the facts and ideas the author gives.

Use your own knowledge.

Use new information that may cause you to change your mind.

Predictions:
_____
_____
_____
_____

Prediction Chart

What characters have we met so far?	What is the conflict in the story?	What are your predictions?	Why did you make those predictions?

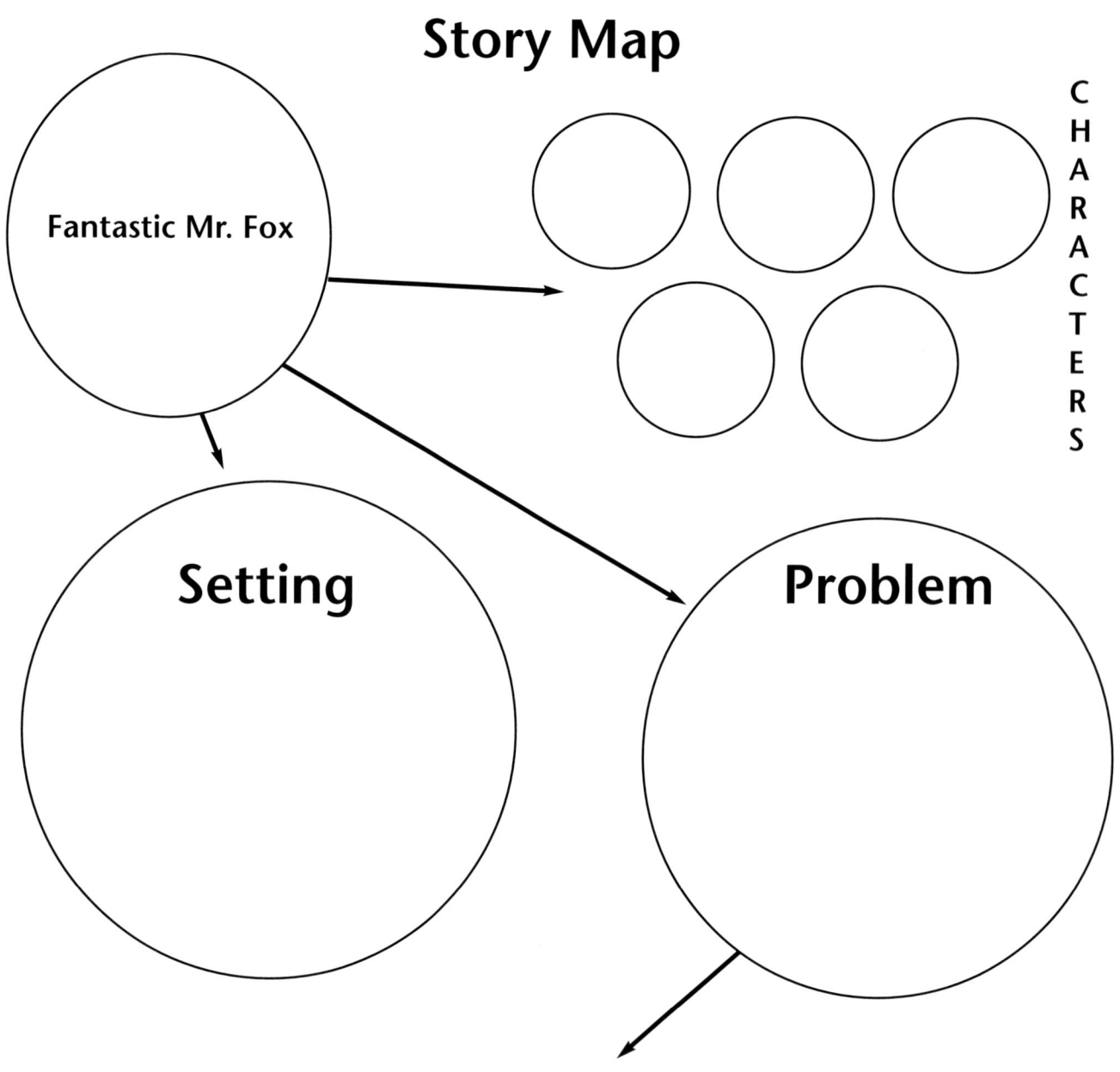

Using Character Webs—In the Novel Unit Approach

Attribute Webs are simply a visual representation of a character from the novel. They provide a systematic way for the students to organize and recap the information they have about a particular character. Attribute webs may be used after reading the novel to recapitulate information about a particular character or completed gradually as information unfolds, done individually, or finished as a group project.

One type of character attribute web uses these divisions:

- How a character acts and feels. (How does the character feel in this picture? How would you feel if this happened to you? How do you think the character feels?)

- How a character looks. (Close your eyes and picture the character. Describe him to me.)

- Where a character lives. (Where and when does the character live?)

- How others feel about the character. (How does another specific character feel about our character?)

In group discussion about the student attribute webs and specific characters, the teacher can ask for backup proof from the novel. You can also include inferential thinking.

Attribute webs need not be confined to characters. They may also be used to organize information about a concept, object or place.

Attribute Web

The attribute web below is designed to help you gather clues the author provides about what a character is like. Fill in the blanks with words and phrases which tell how the character acts and looks, as well as what the character says and what others say about him or her.

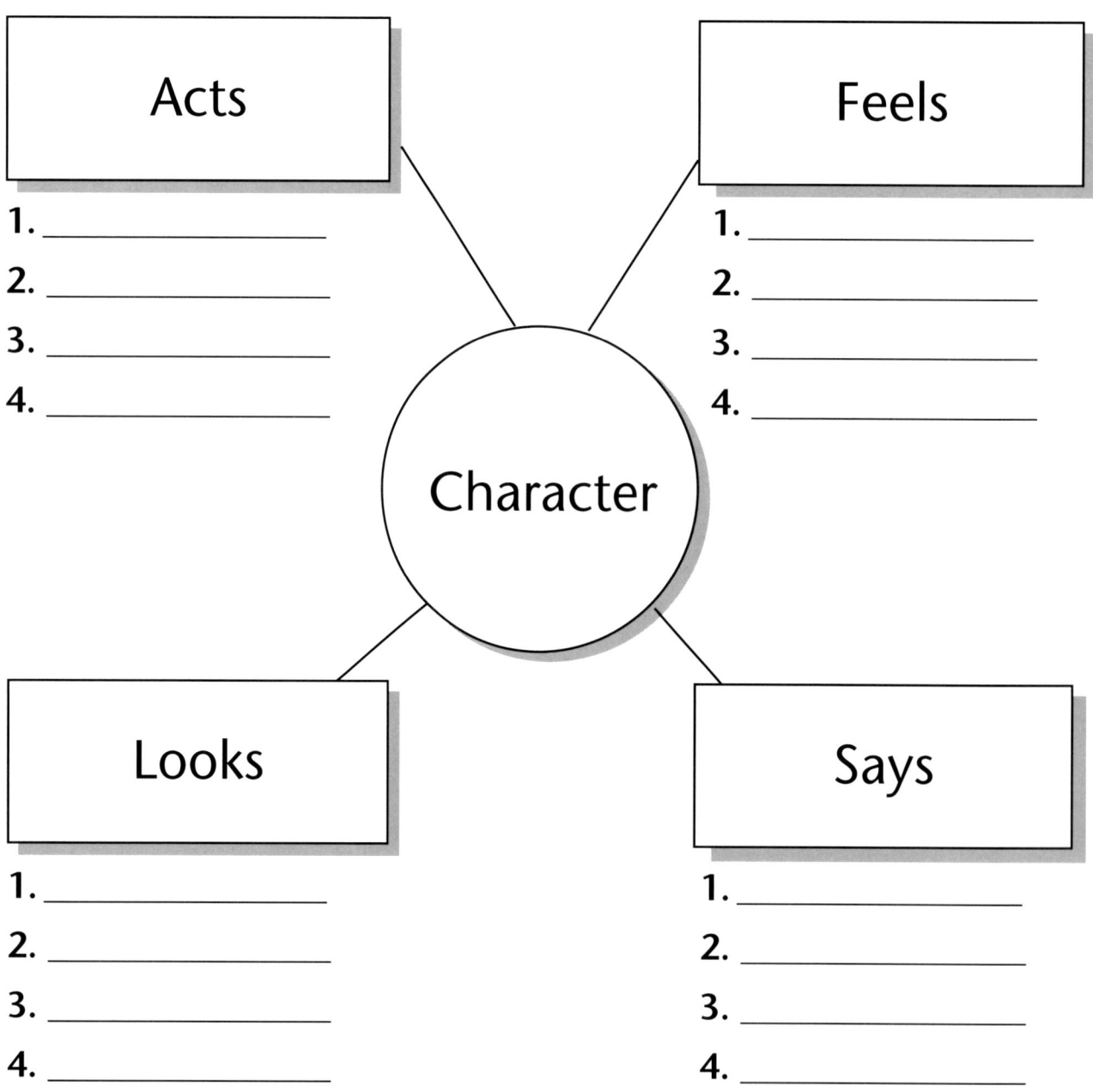

Acts
1. _____
2. _____
3. _____
4. _____

Feels
1. _____
2. _____
3. _____
4. _____

Looks
1. _____
2. _____
3. _____
4. _____

Says
1. _____
2. _____
3. _____
4. _____

© Novel Units, Inc. All rights reserved

Attribute Web

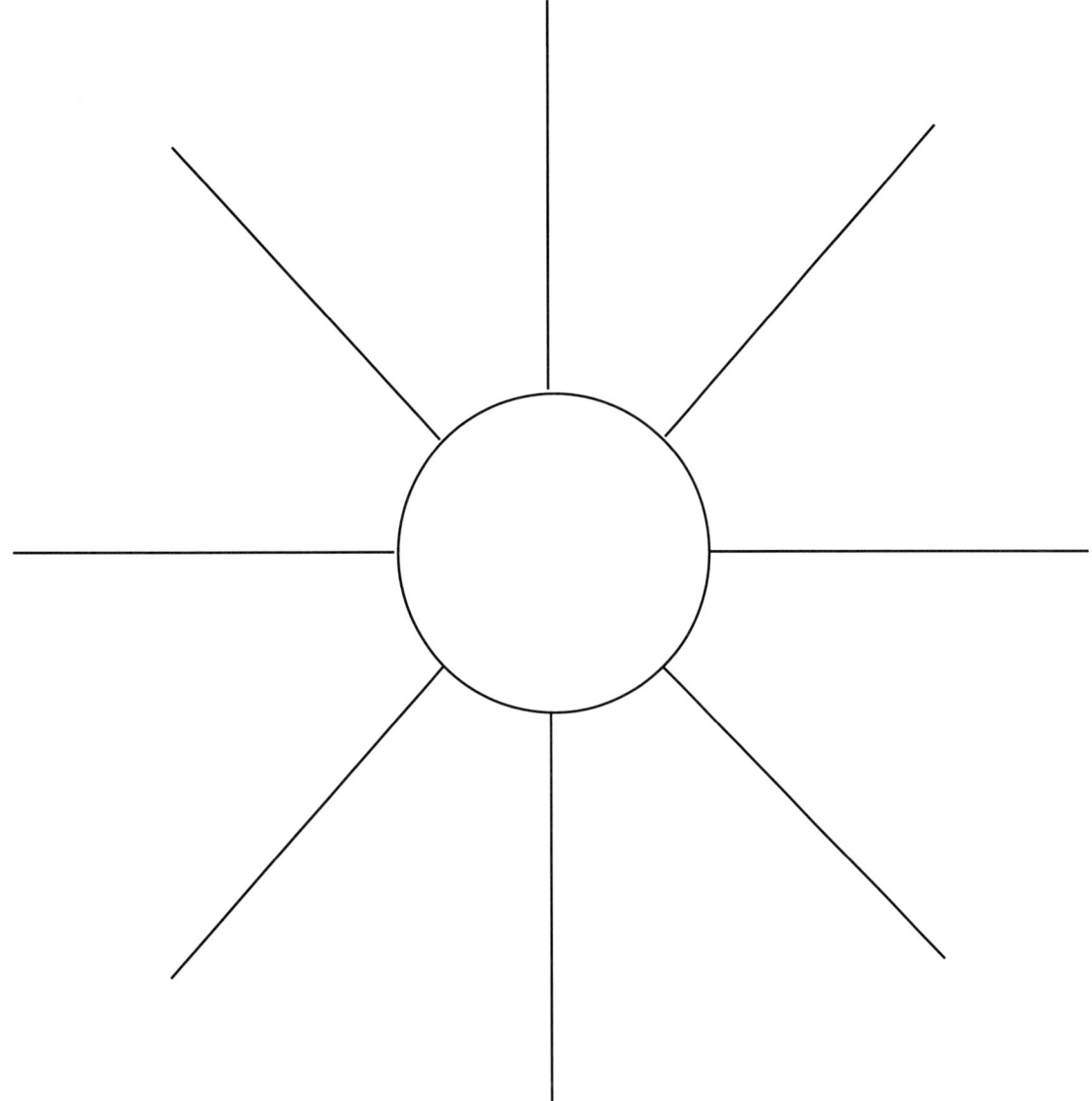

Vocabulary Activities

1. Using the vocabulary lists in this guide, pronounce selected words for a particular section of the book. Have students fill out a chart like the following. They should predict the definition based on the way the word sounds, read the word in context, discuss context clues with others in the class, and jot down the dictionary definition that fits the way the word is used in the book.

Word	Prediction	Dictionary Definition

2. Have students show knowledge of words before reading the chapter by writing simple definitions in their own words of the vocabulary words listed on the board or activity sheet. These short definitions may be developed by individual students or cooperative groups. It is all right to make guesses using root or base words. After reading, ask students to redefine the words referring to the text and/or dictionary.

Vocabulary Words	I Can Define	I Have Heard	I Don't Know

3. Have students "map" selected words that fit into the following framework:

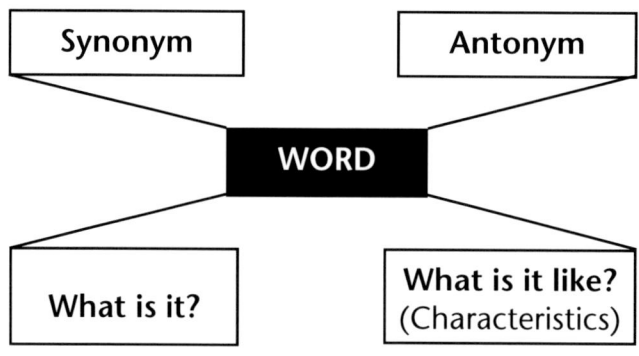

What are some examples?
(verbal, pictorial, or concrete)

4. Words in Context: Ask students to "guess" at the meaning from context, telling why for each guess. Make a list of "why answers" to teach context clues.

5. Have students act out some of the words on the list and see if classmates can guess the target words. For example, students might try to demonstrate "rage," "lurking," or "crouching."

6. Vocabulary Challenge: Use the words from several chapters. The students work in pairs. One student picks a word from the list. Another student has ten (or five) questions to discover the word and give the definition.

7. Crossword Puzzles: Have students use vocabulary words from the chapter to make crossword puzzles on graph paper. They should write a question for each word and develop an answer sheet. The teacher will check and then distribute the puzzles to other students to work.

8. Assign one word to each of five cooperative groups, or one word per student. Each student or cooperative group should make a poster, banner or sign to advertise their word. The ad must show what the word means and how to pronounce it. The ads should be displayed and should be signed.

9. Find the base or root word for each vocabulary word. What prefixes or suffixes were added? What is the meaning of the root word? How did the prefix or suffix change the root word? What is the origin of the word?

10. Put the vocabulary words for a chapter or section in alphabetical order. Arrange the words into sets of two. Use each set of words in the same sentence.

Author's Craft

Roald Dahl uses many techniques that capture the reader and which make *Fantastic Mr. Fox* a memorable literary experience. As the students read the novel, call attention to what the author is doing and why he is using these.

Characterization:
Characterization is the way an author informs readers about what characters are like. Direct characterization is when the author describes the character. Indirect characterization is when the reader figures out what the character is like based on what the character thinks, says, or does.

Ask—What words and phrases are used to describe the three farmers? *(pages 8-13, nasty, mean, beastly temper, clever)* This is *direct characterization.*

Ask—How do we know what kind of character Mr. Fox is? *(pages 29-24, how he talks to his wife, what he thinks about getting food for his family, and how he outsmarts the farmers)* This is *indirect characterization.*

As the story continues, students may find additional examples of characterization.

Conflict:
Conflict is a struggle or problem that makes a story interesting. There are several types of conflict: 1) a person against another person, 2) a person against nature or society, and 3) inner conflict, in which a character struggles with his or her own feelings. Ask students to find an example of each type of conflict in *Fantastic Mr. Fox*.

Suspense:
Explain that suspense is a story quality that produces tension in the reader. The reader grows curious about what will happen next. Suspense usually raises one or two types of questions in a reader's mind: (1) What will the outcome be? and (2) When will the inevitable outcome happen? Have students discuss how suspense develops in each section. (The reader wants to know, first—Are the farmers a threat? and later—Will Mr. Fox outwit the farmers?) Explain that suspense often depends on (1) uncertainty about which of two opposing forces will win—or how, and (2) desire to see one force defeat the other. Ask: Who do you want to win—the farmers or Mr. Fox? Do you want the farmers to succeed in killing Mr. Fox or in starving the Fox family? Why?

Atmosphere or Mood:
Explain that the atmosphere is the overall mood—the dominant emotional tone of a literary work. Atmosphere is created by the handling of setting, character, and theme.

It is often described by adjectives such as:

>page 16, "creep down into the valley in the darkness of the night and help himself."
>page 17, "take his shotgun and hide in a dark place…hoping to catch the robber."
>page 23, "The wood was murky and very still."

Ask students how they would describe the atmosphere. How has Dahl developed this atmosphere? For example, what words convey a sense of danger for the Fox family?

You might put the following chart on the board as you elicit suggestions about how the author creates a menacing atmosphere.

Page	Phrases to Describe Setting	Phrases to Describe Farmers or Mr. Fox	Tone

Climax:
Explain that the climax of a story is the point at which the conflict reaches its highest intensity and the reader's emotional response is at its greatest point.

>Ask: What was the climax of this story? *(page 45, The Foxes Begin to Starve)*
>Was it a surprise or was it predictable? Did the story end with the climax or go on to a resolution?

Theme:
Theme is an important idea that emerges from a story. Authors usually don't state the theme of a work outright, but let their readers decide for themselves what ideas in the story are most important. For clues to theme, readers can look at the characters, the main events, and the conflicts in a story. You should also take a close look at what the main characters learn and how they change from the beginning of the story to the end. Most stories have several themes.

At the conclusion of the novel, brainstorm some possible themes of *Fantastic Mr. Fox*. The following diagram and the list should help you get started.

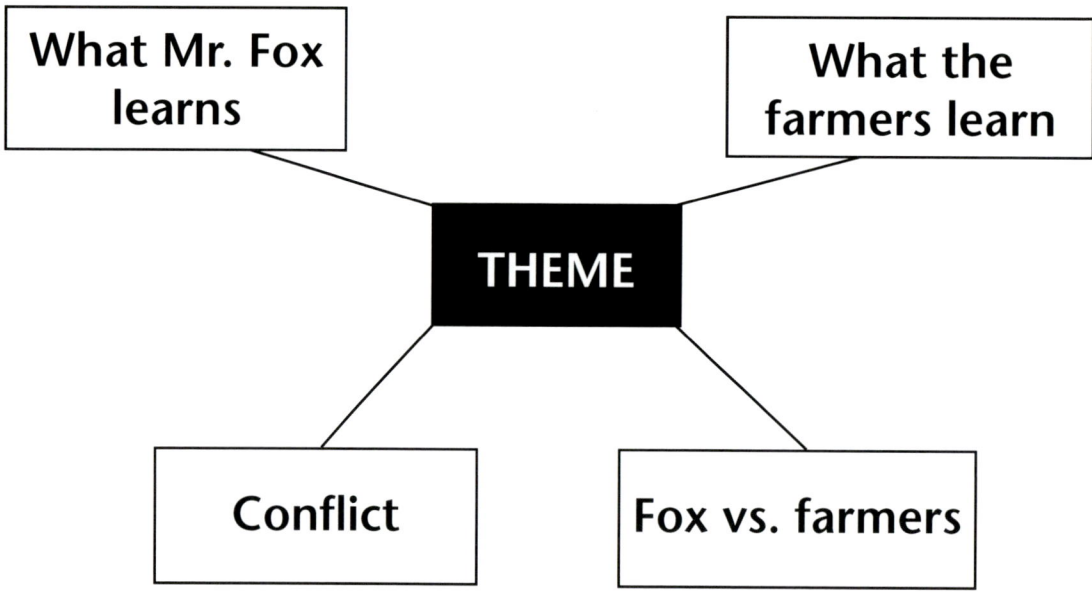

What issues did the author raise for you?

Some Universal Themes
- courage
- survival
- family relationships
- kindness
- values

Chapter-by-Chapter Vocabulary, Discussion Questions, and Activities

Chapter 1: "The Three Farmers" — Pages 8-14

Vocabulary:
    enormously 8   smothered 8

Discussion Questions and Activities:
1. Memorize the song the children used to sing when they saw the three farmers.

   > Boggis and Bunce and Bean
   > One fat, one short, one lean.
   > These horrible crooks
   > So different in looks
   > Were nonetheless equally mean.

2. Fill out the chart on page 12 of this guide.

Chapter 2: "Mr. Fox" — Pages 15-20

Vocabulary:
rage 17	clever 18	approached 18	lurking 18
lousy 18	blighter 18	crafty 20	

Discussion Questions and Activities:
1. How did Mr. Fox outsmart the farmers? *(Page 18, He always approached a farm with the wind blowing in his face, and this meant that if any man was lurking in the shadows ahead, the wind would carry the smell of that man to Mr. Fox's nose from far away.)*

2. Begin an attribute web for Mr. Fox. (See pages 11-13 of this guide.)

Prediction:
Will the farmers kill Mr. Fox?

Chapter 3: "The Shooting" — Pages 21-24

Vocabulary:
goons 21	reeks 21	poisonous 21	cocky 21
crouching 21	murky 23	flask 24	

The Three Farmers

Farmer	Favorite Food	Shape of Body	Type of Farmer
Farmer Boggis			
Farmer Bunce			
Farmer Bean			

Look at the illustrations of the three farmers in Chapter 1. Illustrate and label each of the farmers below.

Discussion Questions and Activities:
1. How did Mr. Fox know the difference between the three farmers? *(Page 21, They each smelled differently.)* Add to the attribute webs for the three farmers.

2. What gave the three farmers away? *(page 23, soft rustling sound, silver speck of moonlight shining on a polished surface, barrel of a gun moving up)*

3. How would Mr. Fox manage without a tail? Is he seriously injured? *(page 24)*

4. Why won't the farmers wait until Mr. Fox comes out of his hole again? *(Page 24, They think it might be three days before Mr. Fox peeks out.)*

Prediction:
Will the farmers find and kill the entire family?

Chapter 4: "The Terrible Shovels"   Pages 25-30

Vocabulary:
glum 25   quivering 26   scrunch 27   electric effect 29

Discussion Questions and Activities:
1. Do you think Mr. Fox's tail will grow back? What does he think? *(page 25)*

2. When they heard the scraping of the shovels, what was Mrs. Fox's first thought? *(Page 27, The farmers would kill her children.)*

3. What did the author mean by, "The sight of this awful thing seemed to have an electric effect upon Mr. Fox"? *(Page 29, Mr. Fox had a bright idea.)*

4. How did Mr. Fox feel when the family had stopped digging? *(Page 30, He thought the farmers would never dig as deep as their tunnel.)*

5. Why did Mrs. Fox say the father is a fantastic fox? *(Page 30, If it were not for Mr. Fox, they would all be dead.)*

Prediction:
Will the farmers give up?

Chapter 5: "The Terrible Tractors"   Pages 31-35

Vocabulary:
mechanical 32   machinery 32   enormous 34   caterpillar 34
murderous 34   brutal 34   toppled 34

Discussion Questions and Activities:
1. Why can't Bean hear? *(Page 31, He never took a bath. His ear holes were clogged.)*

2. How did the author describe the mechanical shovels? *(page 34, black, murderous, brutal-looking monsters)*

3. How do you think the Fox Family felt when the tractors started to dig? *(page 35, afraid, terrified)*

Chapter 6: "The Race"   Pages 36-40

Vocabulary:

desperate 36	keen 39	prowling 39	maniacs 39
dervish 39	crater 40	extraordinary 40	jeered 40
furious 40	obstinate 40	determined 40	

Discussion Questions and Activities:
1. When the Fox Family heard only the faint noises of the tractor, why were they hopeful? *(Page 38, They thought that they might not be captured and killed by the farmers.)*

2. Look at the picture on page 38. How much of the hill is there? How much of the hill is on page 39?

3. How did the author describe the farmers? *(page 39, mad, maniacs, dervish)*

4. How did the author describe the hole pictured on page 39? *(page 40, like the crater of a volcano)*

5. What did the people of the village think of the farmers? *(Page 40, They were mad.)* What does the word *mad* mean? *(crazy)*

Prediction:
What will the farmers try next?

Chapter 7: "We'll Never Let Him Go"   Pages 41-44

Vocabulary:
      solemn 42

Discussion Questions and Activities:
1. How did the farmers demonstrate to each other that they wouldn't give up? *(Page 42, They shook hands.)*
2. What was the farmers' plan? *(Page 43, Their plan was to starve them out. They were going to camp there day and night.)*

Prediction:
Do you think this plan will work? Why or why not?

Chapter 8: "The Foxes Begin to Starve"   Pages 45-47

Vocabulary:
    wafted 45

Discussion Questions and Activities:
1. How long has the Fox Family been without food? *(at least one day and two nights)*
2. How long have you ever been without food or water? How did you feel?
3. Was the Fox Family tempted to take the farmers' food? How do you know? *(Page 46, "Oh Dad, …couldn't we just sneak up and snatch it out of his hand?")*
4. How did the farmers get the men who work for them to help? *(Pages 46-47, The men—108 of them—formed a ring around the hill.)*
5. How was Mr. Fox sure the farmers were still there? *(Page 47, Bean stinks.)*

Prediction:
What will the Fox Family try next? Will the farmers starve them out of the tunnel?

Chapter 9: "Mr. Fox Has a Plan"   Pages 48-50

Vocabulary:
    desperately 49   undefeated 49

Discussion Questions and Activities:
1. What was happening to the Fox Family after three days and three nights? *(Page 48, They were slowly but surely starving to death.)*
2. How did Mrs. Fox feel about letting her children out? *(Page 49, "I refuse to let you go up there and face those guns. I'd sooner you stay down here and die in peace.")*

Prediction:
Look at the illustration and title on page 51. What do you think Mr. Fox's plan is?

Chapter 10: "Boggis's Chicken House Number One" Pages 51-56

Vocabulary:
    marvellous 52   cautiously 53   shriek 53   prancing 55
    clever 55   trough 55

Discussion Questions and Activities:
1. Do you think it was wise of Mr. Fox to not tell his children where they were going while digging? *(Page 52, "…if we failed to get there…you would die of disappointment.")*

2. How did Mr. Fox show his excitement when they got to the place he was hoping for? *(Page 55, "He…started prancing and dancing with joy.")*

3. How did the little foxes act when they first got into the chicken house? *(Page 55, They started running around in all directions, chasing chickens.)*

4. What did Mr. Fox mean when he said, "Let's do this properly"? *(Page 55, "First…have a drink of water. Then Mr. Fox chose three of the plumpest hens, and with a clever flick of his jaws he killed them instantly.")*

Prediction:
What other arrangement will Mr. Fox make?

Chapter 11: "A Surprise for Mrs. Fox" Pages 57-58

Vocabulary:
    Mummy 57   spluttered 58   plucking 58

Discussion Questions and Activities:
1. What was Mrs. Fox's reaction when she first saw the chickens? *(Page 58, "I'm dreaming.")*

2. How did Mrs. Fox feel about preparing a feast? *(page 58, gave her new strength, started her son plucking the chickens, said, "…what a fantastic fox your father is")*

Prediction:
Why is Mr. Fox digging another tunnel?

© Novel Units, Inc.   All rights reserved

Chapter 12: "Badger"   Pages 59-62

Vocabulary:
whacking 59	churgle 59	foggiest 59	chaos 59
furiously 61	unfortunately 61	galore 61	assure 61

Discussion Questions and Activities:
1. List all the animals who were starving. *(page 60, Mole, Rabbit, Weasel, Badger, and their wives and children)*

2. How are all these animals alike? How are they different? Research. *(They all dig underground. Their food differs.)*

3. Why did Mr. Badger say that everyone is starving because of Mr. Fox? *(Pages 60-61, Men were running over the countryside. No one could get out—even at night.)*

4. Even though Mr. Fox's family was starving, he decided to have a feast and invited all the other animals. What descriptive words can we add to Mr. Fox's attribute web?

Prediction:
What could go wrong at such a feast? Will the feast be successful?

Chapter 13: "Bunce's Giant Storehouse"   Pages 63-69

Vocabulary:
slyly 64	gaped 65	paradise 65	grub 65
ravenously 65	luscious 65	morsels 67	magnificent 67
trolley 68			

Discussion Questions and Activities:
1. What was the purpose of Bunce's storehouse? *(Page 65, He stored his finest stuff in there before he sent it off to market.)*

2. Why did Mr. Fox tell everyone to be neat and orderly while taking the food? *(Page 67, "Mustn't let them know what we've been up to.")*

3. Why did Mr. Fox tell his son that he was thoughtful? *(Pages 67-68, The rabbits eat only vegetables.)*

Prediction:
What could "one more little job" be?

Chapter 14: "Badger Has Doubts" Pages 70-72

Vocabulary:
    dotty 71   frump 71   respectable 71

Discussion Questions and Activities:
1. How did Badger feel about taking food? *(Page 71, He called it stealing.)* What does *stealing* mean?

2. How did Mr. Fox justify taking chickens? What does *justify* mean? *(Page 71, Justify means to demonstrate to be just or right. "…who wouldn't swipe a few chickens if their children were starving to death?")*

3. How did Mr. Fox convince Badger? *(Page 71, He said Badger was too respectable; the animals were not going to stoop to the level of the farmers; "We shall simply take a little food here and there to keep our families alive"; "We down here are decent peace-loving people"—contrasted to the farmers who were killers.)*

4. Role Play: Mr. Fox convincing Badger to steal.

5. Writing: Are you on the human side—the farmers—or on Mr. Fox's side? Justify your vote in two to three sentences.

Chapter 15: "Bean's Secret Cider Cellar" Pages 73-77

Vocabulary:
    saucy 74   brilliant 74   peered 74   accustomed 74
    tremendous 75   home-brewed 75   liquor 75   fabulous 75
    poaching 77

Discussion Questions and Activities:
1. What did the Rat mean when he said, "This is my private pitch"? *(It was his territory.)*

2. How did Mr. Fox get Rat out of the way? *(Page 74, "I am a hungry fellow and if you don't hop it quickly I shall eat-you-up-in-one-gulp!")*

Prediction:
Will the animals get caught?

Chapter 16: "The Woman" Pages 78-81

Vocabulary:
  brute 80 souvenir 80

Discussion Questions and Activities:
1. Why do you think the woman carried a rolling pin with her?

2. What did Mrs. Bean promise that the woman could have as a souvenir? *(Page 80, "You can have the head…You can get it stuffed and hang it on your bedroom wall.")* Would you like this kind of souvenir? Why or why not?

3. Do you think that Rat should have called Fox and Badger thieves? Explain. *(Rat, too, is taking what does not belong to him.)*

Chapter 17: "The Great Feast" Pages 82-88

Vocabulary:
  impudent 82 ravenous 84 succulent 84 courtesy 86
  Messrs. 86 colossal 86 marvelous 87

Discussion Questions and Activities:
1. What did Mr. Fox mean by, "This delicious meal, my friends,…is by courtesy of Messrs. Boggis, Bunce, and Bean"? *(By courtesy was Mr. Fox's joke. He had stolen all the food from the farmers' storehouses.)*

2. Do you think it was a good idea for all the animals to live underground forever and never go outside again? Why or why not?

3. Do you think that the animals will always be able to go shopping like they did for the feast?

Prediction:
How is this story going to end?

Chapter 18: "Still Waiting"   Pages 89-90

Vocabulary:
    famished 90

Discussion Questions and Activities:
1. Look at the illustration on page 89. What do you think *each* farmer is thinking?

2. How long do you think Boggis, Bunce, and Bean will wait for Mr. Fox to emerge from his fox hole? How long would you wait?

3. TV: With a partner, illustrate all of the chapters from the book. Use long white paper glued to dowels on either end. Fit into a cardboard box (TV).

Postreading Questions

1. Summarize the story using the story diagram below. What purpose is there in a story diagram? How would using a story diagram help an author?

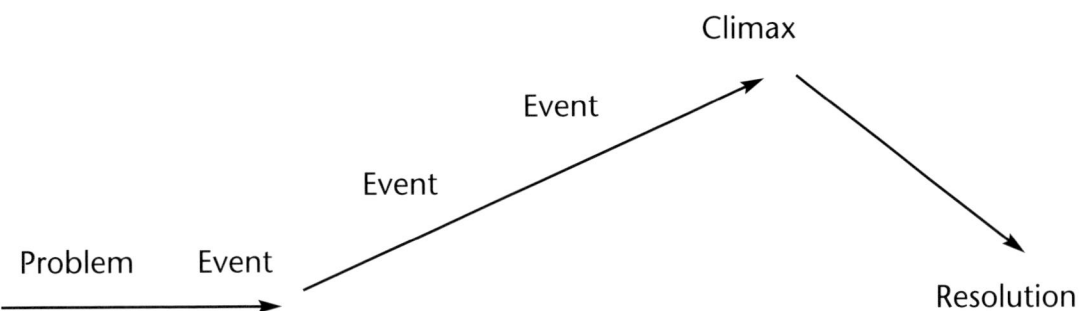

2. Characterization: Characters are developed by what they say, think, and do and by how others in the novel react to them. Review the attribute webs. Which character or characters provided wisdom and perspective? How did the characters change during the story? How would you explain the changes?

    Would you agree that Mr. Fox is fantastic? Why or why not?

    How does the author make you like Mr. Fox and dislike the farmers? (The farmers are pictured as not very nice people—smelly, mean, nasty, beastly. Mr. Fox is pictured as charming, hardworking, a good father, clever and a hero.)

    Complete the attribute webs for the farmers and for Mr. Fox.

    Do the animals in the novel act like real animals? How does the author personify the animals or make them seem like people?

3. Plot: In literature the plot often is carried along by causes and effects of decision made by the main characters. Had a character made an alternate decision, the plot would have turned in a different direction. What were the important decisions or turning points of this story?

4. Theme is the novel's central idea. What is this author's message? Why do you think the author wrote this story? What do you think is the most important thing to remember about this story? Support your ideas for the theme or themes with examples from the novel. Is the central theme of this story presented directly or indirectly?

Postreading Extension Activities

Writing Activities:
1. Write a diary entry for one day that each of the main characters might write.

2. Pick one of the characters in the novel and write five questions that you would like to ask in order to understand the way he acted in the story.

3. Add another chapter to the novel involving the same characters that would make the story more exciting.

4. How important is the setting to the story? (In what time and place is the story set?) How do the various settings contribute to the mood and move the plot along?

5. An epilogue is an addition to a story that tells what happened later. Choose a time in the future and write a brief epilogue to the activities of Mr. Fox and the farmers.

Listening and Speaking Activities:
1. Stage a TV interview with some of the characters in the story. For homework, students playing each role gather impressions about what their character is like. Other students make lists of interview questions.

2. Retell an episode from your favorite chapter from the viewpoint of another character, e.g. Mrs. Fox or Rat.

3. Work with a partner to write an imaginary dialogue between yourself and one of the characters in the novel. The character you choose should act and respond in the same manner as he or she does in the novel. With your partner, present your dialogue to the class.

4. Pantomime a scene from the novel.

Art Activities:
1. Mural: Draw and paint a mural of an underground village for Mr. Fox and the other animals. Include:

   —Houses for the foxes;
   the rabbits;
   the badgers;
   the weasels;
   the moles.

—Tunnels for the farmers' houses;
> Bean's cider cellar;
> Bunce's storehouse;
> Boggis's chicken house.

2. Mobile: Choose three scenes from the story. Illustrate each scene on construction paper. Punch a hole at the top of each section. Thread with string. Hang each section at different lengths with a plastic straw. Hang the mobile from the ceiling.

3. Draw a picture of the Fox Family or the three farmers.

4. Create a picture of a scene from the novel. Some suggestions: the farmers shooting Mr. Fox's tail or the farmers digging into the Foxes' home.

5. Make a collage on a large piece of poster board. Divide the poster board into sections. Each section should represent a character in the story. You may use magazine cut-outs and drawings of your own.

Using Dialogue

Directions: Choose a bit of dialogue from the book to investigate. Fill in the chart to describe this way of writing and telling a story.

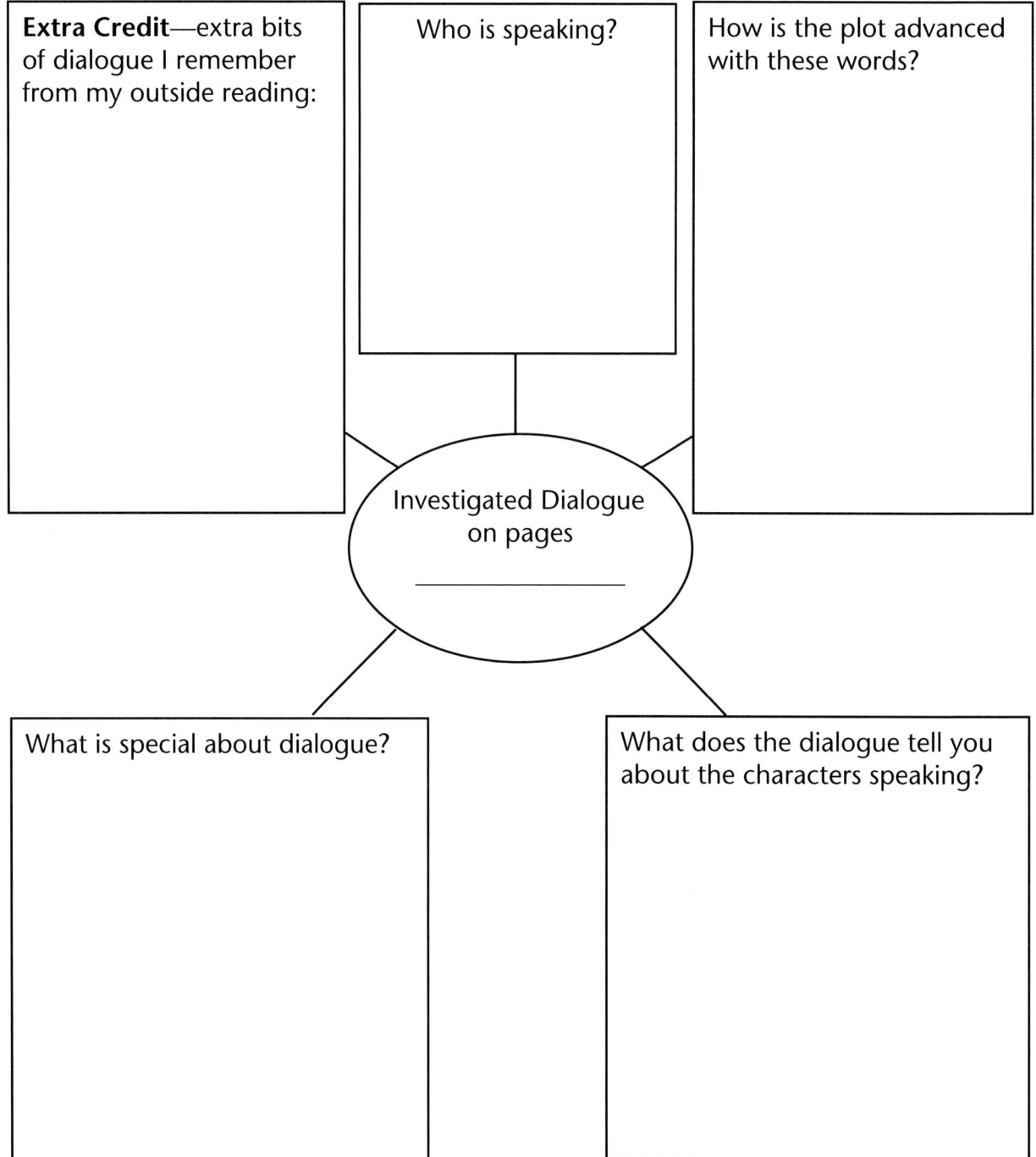

- **Extra Credit**—extra bits of dialogue I remember from my outside reading:
- Who is speaking?
- How is the plot advanced with these words?
- Investigated Dialogue on pages _____
- What is special about dialogue?
- What does the dialogue tell you about the characters speaking?

Cause-Effect Maps

To plot cause and effect in a story, first list the sequence of events. Then mark the causes with a **C** and effects with an **E**. Use an arrow from the cause to the effect. Remember that many effects cause something else so they might be marked with an **E** and a **C** with an arrow to the next effect.

Events in the Story

1.
2.
3.
4.
5.
6.
7.
8.
9.
10.

Another way to map cause and effect is to look for an effect and then backtrack to the single or multiple causes.

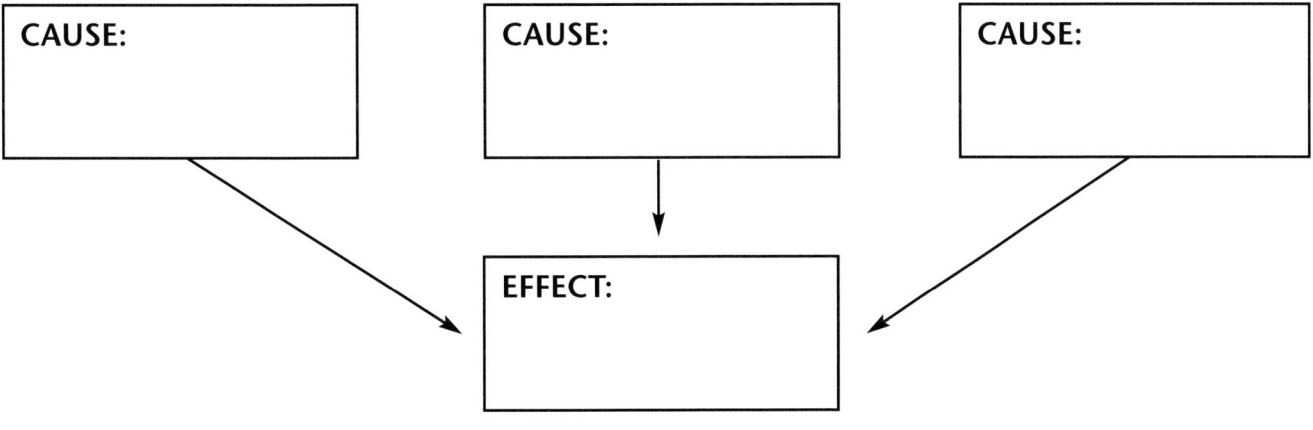

Cause and Effect

> When something happens that causes something else to happen, the first event is called a *cause*.

> The event that happens as a result of something else is called an *effect*.

Example:

Cause: Mr. Fox crept out of his hole for food.

Effect: (The result—what happened?) The farmers shot off his tail.

Directions: Read each cause below and write its effect.

CAUSE (An event)	EFFECT (The result—what happened?)
1. At the beginning of the story, the farmers agree that Mr. Fox is a nuisance.	1.
2. The farmers used mechanical shovels.	2.
3. The foxes were trapped in their hole.	3.
4. The animals took chickens, ducks, geese, and cider.	4.
5. Mr. Fox made sure the animals would never be without food.	5.

Simile

Sometimes an author uses a simile (sim-a-lee) to help the reader form an image. A *simile* is a comparison between two things. A simile usually uses *like* or *as*.

Directions: Read the simile in the left column. Illustrate it in the right column.

Simile	Illustration (What do you imagine?)
1. "He [Bean] was *as* thin *as* a pencil." (page 13)	1.
2. "…were driving their machines *like* maniacs…" (page 39)	2.
3. "The hole the machines had dug was *like* the crater of a volcano." (page 40)	3.
4. "Their [Small Foxes'] eyes shining *like* stars." (page 68)	4.
5. "It's…it's [cider] *like* melted gold!" (page 75)	5.
6. "And every day we [foxes] will eat *like* kings." (page 88)	6.

Assessment for *Fantastic Mr. Fox*

Assessment is an on-going process, more than a quiz at the end of the book. Points may be added to show the level of achievement. When an item is completed, the teacher and the student check it.

Name _____ Date _____

Student   Teacher

_____   _____   1. Make attribute webs for the major characters.

_____   _____   2. Give yourself one point for each vocabulary activity completed.

_____   _____   3. Make a four-panel cartoon strip of an important incident in the novel and quote conversation from the novel in balloons above the speakers.

_____   _____   4. Compare Mr. Fox to the farmers using a T-Diagram.

_____   _____   5. Write three questions about the novel and participate in a small group discussion of these and other student generated questions.

_____   _____   6. Do a small group dramatization of a scene in the story.

_____   _____   7. Make your own type of story map.

_____   _____   8. What is a hero? Is Mr. Fox a hero? First, list all the characteristics of a hero. If you think Mr. Fox is a hero, list how he demonstrates heroic qualities. Be specific. If you do not think he is a hero, tell what is missing.

_____   _____   9. How could the ending of the novel be changed? Write a new ending and be ready to justify why your ending is better than the author's.

_____   _____   10. Select your best writing project and polish it to share with classmates.

© Novel Units, Inc.   All rights reserved